ALEXANDER THE GREAT AND THE GREEKS

Nathaniel Harris

Illustrated by Gerry Wood

LIFE AND TIMES

Alexander the Great and the Greeks
Julius Caesar and the Romans
Alfred the Great and the Saxons
Canute and the Vikings
William the Conqueror and the Normans
Richard the Lionheart and the Crusades
Columbus and the Age of Exploration
Montezuma and the Aztecs
Elizabeth I and Tudor England
Oliver Cromwell and the Civil War
Pepys and the Stuarts
Daniel Boone and the American West

Further titles are in preparation

First published in 1985 by
Wayland (Publishers) Ltd
49 Lansdowne Place, Hove
East Sussex BN3 1HF, England

© Copyright 1985 Wayland (Publishers) Ltd

ISBN 0 85078 574 X

Phototypeset by Planagraphic Typesetters Ltd
Printed in Italy by G. Canale & C.S.p.A., Turin
Bound in the U.K. by The Pitman Press, Bath

Contents

1 ALEXANDER, TYRANT OF GENIUS

The northern kingdom

In the fourth century BC, the Greeks had a flourishing civilization of which they were understandably proud. They excelled as statesmen, builders, sculptors, poets, dramatists and philosophers. And although Greece was divided into many small states, the Greeks had won great victories on land and sea, fighting off two invasions by the mighty Persian Empire.

Above *A sculpted head of Alexander.*

But all too often the Greek states (see map on page 27) wasted their strength by quarrelling among themselves. Eventually a strong and determined ruler took advantage of this situation, picking off the disunited Greek states one by one until he controlled them all. This ruler was Philip II, King of Macedon in northern Greece. Most Greeks thought of the Macedonians as wild frontiersmen, so uncivilized that they hardly counted as true Greeks. But Philip turned his tough frontiersmen into efficient professional soldiers, and gradually made Macedon the dominant power in Greece.

These things were happening during the childhood of Philip's son Alexander, who was born at the Macedonian capital, Pella, in 356 BC. Although his teacher was Aristotle, a famous and studious Greek philosopher, Alexander's warlike nature soon became apparent. When he was only eight he tamed Bucephalus, a horse no one else had managed to ride; it was to be his mount in most of his battles. At 16 years old Alexander was regent of Macedon while his father was away. And at the battle of Chaeronaea (338 BC) he led the left flank of the Macedonian army which crushed the last Greek resistance.

Left *The young Alexander tames Bucephalus, his favourite horse.*

Above *Alexander's troops take revenge on the city of Thebes, burning it down and selling the people into slavery.*

Alexander strikes

After Chaeronaea, the Greek states were forced to recognize Philip of Macedon as their leader. Philip now prepared to launch a Greek attack on Persia, the traditional enemy. The Persian Empire was vast, taking in the entire Middle East and Egypt, but Greeks had beaten Persians often enough in the past to face a war with confidence.

But first there was a crisis in the Macedonian royal family. Philip suddenly divorced Alexander's mother, Olympias, and took a new wife. Alexander fell from favour and even went into exile for a time. He was soon allowed to return, but he must have wondered whether he

would ever inherit the throne. Then, in 336 BC, Philip was murdered by one of his own bodyguards, and Alexander did become king. Whether or not he was behind Philip's murder will never be known for certain.

Philip's unwilling allies among the Greeks rejoiced at his death — too soon. Alexander swept into Greece at lightning speed and cowed his 'allies' into submission. Soon afterwards, when he was campaigning in the far north, the Greek states again tried to recover their independence, only to be defeated again. This time Alexander revenged himself: the ancient city of Thebes was utterly destroyed and its people sold into slavery. Alexander stood revealed as a military genius — and also a ruthless tyrant. Master of Greece, he was now ready to take on the Persians.

The god-king

In the spring of 334 BC Alexander crossed the Hellespont (the narrow strip of water separating Europe from Asia) and landed on Persian territory. In May his army of 40,000 had its first serious test when the local satrap (regional governor) took up a strong position with his troops on the banks of the River Granicus. Alexander's men showed their spirit by fording the river and overwhelming the Persian forces.

On his march through Asia Minor (modern Turkey), Alexander stopped at Gordium and was shown the famous Gordian knot. According to the legend, this knot secured the yoke of the chariot of the ancient king Gordias to a post, outside the temple of Zeus. The ends of the knot were hidden. It was said that the man who could untie it would become Lord of Asia. Alexander did untie it — by simply slashing through it with his sword.

Then Darius himself, the 'Great King' of Persia, arrived to face the invader at a place called Issus. Once again the Persians failed to overrun the Macedonian infantry, and broke before the charging cavalry led by Alexander. The Persians, including Darius, fled in disorder, even leaving behind the Great King's mother, wife and children.

Instead of invading Persia at once, Alexander decided to cut his enemies off from the Mediterranean. He occupied Syria and Palestine, brutally destroying the ancient port of Tyre after a seven-month siege. In Egypt he was hailed as the new pharaoh, which made him both king and god — a promotion he seems to have taken quite seriously — and he founded the city of Alexandria on the Mediterranean coast, which still exists.

Below *Egyptian soldiers bow before Alexander, greeting him as the new pharaoh.*

Lord of Asia

In 331 BC Alexander marched back into Asia for a final showdown with Darius. On 30 September their armies clashed at Gaugamela, near the River Tigris. The Macedonians were outnumbered five to one, but Alexander's superb strategy carried the day: the Persians were lured into attacking in strength on the wings, then Alexander and his cavalrymen thrust through their weakened centre and threw them into confusion.

Below *Alexander approaches the corpse of his determined enemy, Darius King of Persia, who was killed by one of his own men.*

The victory was decisive. Darius managed to get away again, but his authority was gone and he was murdered by one of his own satraps. During the next few months Alexander occupied the great cities of the Empire (Babylon, Susa, Persepolis) and made himself the new 'Great King' and Lord of Asia.

As one campaign followed another, Alexander's troops realized with dismay that he would never willingly stop fighting. Having conquered Persia, he went on into India. Even there he was victorious, though his men were frightened by a weapon they had never seen before — the elephant.

Finally, Alexander's men simply refused to go on, and he was forced to return to his capital, Babylon. He was now as much a Persian king as a Greek one, and planned to create a joint Greek-Persian army and ruling class. His behaviour was often cruel and unpredictable: he even killed one of his best friends in a fit of rage. When he died — possibly from poison — he was preparing yet another warlike expedition, to Arabia. By then he was still only 32 years old.

Above *Alexander's army witholds an attack from the enemy in India.*

Below *A bronze statue of a Greek cavalryman.*

Above *Theseus confronts the Minotaur in the labyrinth and eventually kills it. The Minotaur was a mythological beast that was half-man and half-bull. It was the child of Pasiphäe, the king of Crete's wife, and a bull sent to Crete by the gods.*

2 WHO WERE THE GREEKS?

Crete and Mycenae

Mainland Greece was occupied by Greek-speaking peoples from about 1900 BC. But for several centuries the Greeks were far less civilized than their neighbours on the large island of Crete, which boasted many-roomed palaces with sumptuous, colourful decorations. We still do not know how to read Cretan writing, but finds made by archaeologists suggest that Cretan civilization was relaxed and cheerful, and probably depended on trade rather than warfare.

Despite Greek legend, which pictures Crete as the home of a Greek-devouring monster called the Minotaur, the Greeks learned much from the Cretans. As a result they developed a civilization of their own, now known as 'Mycenaean'. The word describes all the Greek kingdoms, which were based on grim stone fortress-towns such as Tiryns and Pylos; Mycenae was the most powerful of these, and its ruler was probably the High King or overlord of the others.

Unlike the Cretans, the Mycenaeans seem to have been extremely warlike, perhaps combining piracy with genuine trade. At any rate they had become wealthy by about 1600 BC, as we can tell from the gold death-masks, richly decorated swords and other objects that they buried with their great men.

Mycenaean Greece flourished until about 1300 BC and then seems to have run into trouble — trouble that may have included the legendary Trojan War.

Above *The Snake Goddess, one of the main goddesses of ancient Crete. She is always shown grasping two serpents.*

Left *Soldiers march into the citadel of Mycenae through the Lion Gate.*

The Trojan War

The Trojan War is legend, not historical fact. The story is told by Homer and other poets of Ancient Greece, all of whom lived centuries after the war is supposed to have taken place. All the same, there are good reasons for supposing that something like the Trojan War did occur in the thirteenth century BC.

The cause of the war is said to have been the beautiful Helen, wife of Menelaus, King of Sparta in southern Greece. Helen ran away with Paris, a prince of Troy, a non-Greek city on the coast of Asia Minor. The Greek kings, led by Menelaus' brother, Agamemnon, High King of Mycenae, were determined to be avenged and sailed with their armies against Troy.

The Greeks are said to have besieged the city for ten years before capturing it by a trick. They pretended to give up the siege and sail away, leaving behind a huge wooden horse. The jubilant Trojans dragged the horse into the city as a prize — but that night, while they slept, Greek warriors emerged from inside the horse and opened the city gates to the returned Greek army. The Trojans, including King Priam and all his sons, were killed or enslaved, and Troy was burned to the ground. The adventurous, often dangerous, return journey is told by the Greek poets. One such epic poem is Homer's *Odyssey*.

This is one of the world's most famous stories. Its details may not all be true, but the war itself may well have happened. In 1870 an archaeologist named Heinrich Schliemann discovered the lost site of Troy, proving that the city had really existed — and that it had been destroyed by fire in the thirteenth century BC!

Above *The design on a Greek vase, showing Menelaus leading Helen back to Sparta.*

Above *Heinrich Schliemann, a nineteenth-century archaeologist who discovered the lost site of Troy.*

Right *The triumphant Trojans pull the wooden horse through the city gate, in the mistaken belief that they had routed the Greeks.*

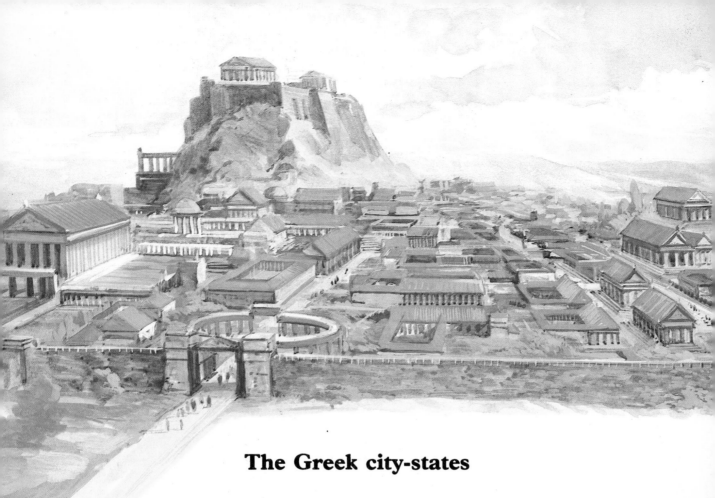

The Greek city-states

By about 1200 BC the Mycenaean world was falling apart. Greece was invaded by a new people, the Dorians, who were also Greek-speaking. A period of wars and migrations followed — a 'Dark Age' in which even the art of writing was lost for several centuries. When the Dark Age ended in about 800 BC, the Dorians and other Greeks had spread beyond Greece to the Aegean islands, Crete, Cyprus and Ionia (now the western coast of Turkey).

The Greeks called the territory they occupied Hellas, and regarded it as their common homeland. They thought of themselves as a single people, the Hellenes — but every Greek was also strongly attached to his little native state, and was only too ready to fight against other Greeks who might threaten it.

During the Dark Age the warlike Mycenaean kingdoms were replaced by smaller units, called city-states. The city-state supported a small population (usually less than 100,000), most of whom were farmers. Its centre was a city, such as Athens or Sparta or Corinth, from which the city-state took its name. Astonishingly, these tiny states created one of the world's great civilizations.

Towards the end of the Dark Age, the Greek population began to increase rapidly. Since the country was not fertile enough to support them, many Greeks left Hellas to found their own cities. They settled in many places around the Mediterranean and the Black Sea, and famous cities such as Syracuse (in Sicily) and Marseille (in France) originated as Greek colonies. Colonization continued until about 550 BC. There were hundreds of new city-states, built on the model of the colonists' home cities. They were like outposts of Greek civilization.

Below *The face and back of an ancient Greek coin, called a drachma. On the face you can see the head of Alexander the Great.*

3 GREECE IN THE CLASSICAL AGE

The rise of Athens

Below The Athenians were great traders, particularly in silver which made them very rich. Mining began at the beginning of the 5th century BC. There was also trade in olive oil and wine; textiles were imported from other parts of Greece.

The ancient Greeks tried out most known types of government, and were the first people to compare them and try to decide which was the best. At one time or another they were ruled by kings, aristocrats (great landowners) and tyrants (dictators who ruled by force rather than legal right). But by about 500 BC — the year which is now thought to mark the beginning of the 'classical' age in Greek history — there were two main forms of government: oligarchies and democracies.

Above *These designs represent the five different forms of government. Monarchy, Tyranny, Aristocracy, Oligarchy and Democracy.*

In oligarchies, control of the government was in the hands of the richer citizens. In democracies, all citizens had the right to take some part in government. Women and slaves were not citizens, so the Greeks' idea of democracy was a limited one; but they must be given credit for inventing it!

The most important of the democracies was Athens, one of the largest and most populous of the Greek states. Athens' pride was her fleet, which enabled her to trade over a wide area. Trade made her rich and brought her into contact with other peoples and new ideas. The Athenians became a lively, curious, argumentative, sometimes unreliable people who produced great literature and works of art. They formed the greatest contrast to their chief rivals — the stern Spartans.

The stern men of Sparta

Below *A 7-year-old boy is taken away from his mother to be trained in the Spartan army.*

Sparta was a completely militarized state, like an army camp on permanent alert. Every Spartan male was a soldier, trained from birth to obey, to endure pain without flinching, and to live simply. Spartans lived mainly in barracks, with no private life, until they reached the age of 30 — even if they were married men. No wonder we still use the word 'spartan' to describe a poorly furnished room or a life without comforts.

The Spartans had adopted this way of life because they were surrounded by enemies inside their own country, and needed to be ready to defend themselves at all times. Sparta was the largest of the Greek states, but the Spartans themselves formed only a minority of the population. The majority were helots (serfs), who served — and hated — their harsh Spartan masters. The helots

were originally farmers, before the Spartans invaded their land, taking half the farm produce for themselves every year. If the Spartans were to keep their power, it was necessary that every Spartan should become a full-time soldier who never relaxed his vigilance.

This made the Spartans fine warriors but rather dull people. Sparta's rulers were afraid of change and kept out new ideas in case they upset their strict system. Not surprisingly, Sparta made no important contribution to the flowering of Greek civilization in the fifth century BC. However, other Greeks — so often quarrelsome and treacherous — did admire the Spartans' discipline and sense of duty, which could inspire them to feats of great heroism.

Sparta championed the cause of oligarchies, while Athens stood for democracy. They were destined to be rivals, though they worked together — with difficulty — when faced by a common foe: the mighty Persians.

Above *Young Spartan boys learned to fight with sword and shield, whatever the weather, at a camp in the mountains. A Spartan's training was very tough.*

The Persian peril

The Persian Empire was expanding rapidly from the 540s, when the Persians conquered all Asia Minor, including the Greek cities of Ionia. Soon afterwards the Persians even added the ancient kingdom of Egypt to their possessions.

The Persians ignored mainland Greece until Ionia rose in revolt, aided by the Athenians. The revolt was put down in 493 BC, and the Persian king, Darius, determined to revenge himself, sent an army to attack Athens. In 490 BC a strong Persian expeditionary force landed on the coast near Marathon. The Athenians sent to Sparta for help, but the Spartans could not set out for six days. Meanwhile, the Athenians, led by the general Miltiades,

Above *The Greeks attack the Persian fleet in the Straits of Salamis. Unlike the Persian ships the Greek ships were designed for ramming, not boarding.*

defeated the Persians. A messenger ran all the way from Marathon to Athens (about 25 miles, or 40 km) with the good news — which is why long-distance races are called marathons to this day.

Ten years later, Darius' son, Xerxes, made a much more serious attempt to conquer Greece, crossing the Hellespont with a huge army. At the narrow pass of Thermopylae the Spartans had their finest hour, while the Greek army made its escape. Leonidas led 300 Spartans and held off the Persian hordes, fighting to the very last man.

Then Xerxes made a fatal mistake. He decided to crush the Greeks at sea, and allowed his large navy to be lured into the straits of Salamis. The Greek fleet, led by the Athenian Themistocles, utterly destroyed the enemy. The victory at Salamis had saved Greece.

Above *Miltiades, the great general who led the Athenians to victory against the Persians at the battle of Marathon.*

The great age of Athens

After the victory at Salamis, the Persians were quickly driven out of Greece. The initiative passed to the Greeks, who raided Persian territory as far afield as Egypt.

In a war mainly fought at sea, Athens inevitably took the lead; the Spartans preferred to stay close to their home territory. They were keen to build up their armies again, after losses at war, to continue their control of the helots. The Greek states that remained active in the war formed an alliance, the Delian League, which was soon dominated by Athens. Gradually the League turned into something that was almost an Athenian empire. Instead of building their own ships, many states in the Delian League were persuaded to give money towards their common defence — which in practice meant making the Athenian fleet even more powerful. The League's funds were kept in the Temple of Apollo on the island of Delos, where the allies met regularly to discuss policy.

Athens was now the strongest, and also the most brilliant, of the Greek city-states. Splendid new temples were built in the city, and it became the chief centre of Greek art and thought. Pericles, her leading statesman, claimed that Athens' free and democratic way of life was largely responsible for her greatness.

The political situation was less bright. The war against Persia ended in 449 BC, but the Delian League remained in being as a permanent Athenian-democratic alliance. It was soon faced by a Peloponnesian League dominated by oligarchic Sparta. Greece was now divided into two hostile power blocs which were bound to clash.

Above *Pericles the Athenian who was largely responsible for the development of Athenian democracy.*

Left *The magnificent gold and ivory statue of Athena in the Parthenon at Athens, which was the temple dedicated to her as the goddess who protected the city.*

The Peloponnesian War

In 431 BC Athens and Sparta became involved in a quarrel between two less important states, Corfu and Corinth, and ended up by declaring war on each other. So began the Peloponnesian War, which lasted (with a seven-year truce in the middle) for twenty-six years.

For a long time it must have seemed that it would never end. The Athenian fleet could do only limited damage to their land-based enemies. And although the Spartans and their allies had the better army, they could not capture Athens itself, since the walls of the city were impregnable, running for 5 miles (8 km) down to the port of Athens, the Piraeus. While Athens had a fleet to supply her she could defy any besieging army.

Two Athenian disasters eventually decided the war. A powerful expedition sent to take Syracuse was encircled and utterly destroyed. Then, a few years later, the Athenian fleet was defeated in the Hellespont. Cut off from vital supplies, Athens was forced to open her gates to the triumphant Spartans.

With limited manpower (and very limited ideas), the Spartans did not make much use of their victory. The Athenians soon managed to regain their independence. But their 'empire' was gone for good, and Sparta's supremacy was even shorter-lived.

Greek civilization continued to flourish, but the Greeks remained as disunited as ever. This was how matters stood all through the fourth century BC . . . until Philip and Alexander of Macedon came on the scene.

Right *A map of Greece showing the main cities, the sites of battles, and temples — including Mount Olympus the home of the gods.*

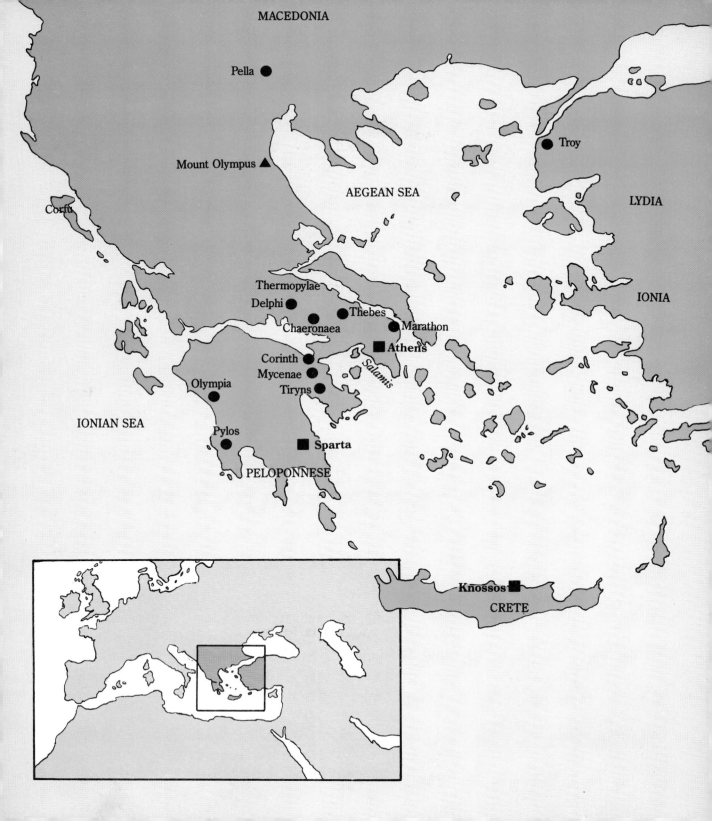

MACEDONIA

Pella ●

Troy ●

Mount Olympus ▲

AEGEAN SEA

LYDIA

Corfu

IONIA

Thermopylae
Delphi ●
Thebes ●
Chaeronaea ●
Marathon ●
Athens ■
Corinth ●
Salamis
Mycenae ●
Olympia ●
Tiryns ●

IONIAN SEA

Pylos ●
Sparta ■

PELOPONNESE

Knossos ■
CRETE

Above *Greek temples were always dedicated to particular gods. The architecture of a temple was grand to suit its purpose.*

Below *An example of beautiful Greek pottery design. It shows Dionysius, the god of wine, and his son.*

4 THE SUPREME ACHIEVEMENT

The arts of Greece

The art and architecture of ancient Greece has deeply influenced our own civilization. Even today, you can walk through many towns and find a building — perhaps a bank or a museum — that imitates the entrance of a Greek temple, with its large triangular feature (pediment) set above a row of columns.

The construction of such buildings was technically quite simple — they are hardly more than stone versions of a flat-topped wooden structure supported by tree trunks. The Greeks never even bothered to use such basic devices as the arch. Yet most of their temples are so beautiful that they have been recognized as masterpieces for over two thousand years. The most famous of them all are the temples on the Acropolis (citadel) of Athens, and especially the Parthenon, dedicated to the protecting goddess of the city, Athena.

In painting and sculpture, earlier civilizations such as Egypt had produced works that were impressive, but stiff, solemn or overpowering. The Greeks aimed to create convincing human beings in marble, bronze and paint. It is difficult now to imagine the wonder with which people must have seen — for the very first time — a sculpted figure of an athlete, muscles straining, about to swing and throw a discus!

No Greek paintings have survived, but we can glimpse something of their quality in the thousands of vivid pictures on Greek pottery. Vases were in great demand and at that time they were not considered to be great works of art.

Below The Greeks made bronze statues in honour of gods and great statesmen. Below left The head of the Greek god of sleep, Hypnos, always shown with two wings growing out of his head.

Gods, myths and oracles

Greek religion was a complicated affair. The Greeks worshipped and sacrificed to a family of gods and goddesses who were said to live on Mount Olympus in northern Greece. Zeus, 'the thunderer', was lord of the skies and king of the gods. Hera was his third wife. Athena was the goddess of wisdom and Aphrodite the goddess of love. Apollo was the god of light, Poseidon the lord of the sea, and Ares the god of war. Beneath the earth, Pluto reigned in the gloomy underworld with his queen, Persephone the daughter of Demeter.

There were many other gods and lesser spirits, as well as heroes such as the strong-man Heracles (Hercules), who all played a part in the Greeks' religious legends.

These legends, properly called myths, have provided writers and artists with a rich fund of stories ever since. Many myths describe quarrels between the gods, who are even supposed to have fought on different sides during the Trojan War! In fact the Greeks seem to have thought of their gods as ordinary and human in everything except their immortality and great strength.

All the same, the Greeks took religion seriously. The holy places were marked by a temple, each of which was dedicated to a particular god. They believed in omens, and looked to oracles for advice — usually a priest or priestess through whom a god was said to speak. Most oracles played safe, and gave advice that could be understood in two different ways. When King Croesus of Lydia asked whether he should fight the Persians, the famous oracle at Delphi said that if he did so 'a great kingdom will be destroyed'. Croesus went to war — but it was his own great kingdom, not the Persians', that was finally destroyed.

Above *The remains of the Temple of Apollo at Delphi.*

Below *Laurel leaves are thrown on a fire in honour of the gods.*

Literature and ideas

The greatest Greek poet was Homer. According to tradition he was blind, but nothing is known of his life, and it is possible that his epic poems, the *Iliad* and the *Odyssey*, are actually the work of several Greek poets. The *Iliad* tells the story of an episode from the Trojan War; the *Odyssey* is a tale of Odysseus's homeward journey from Troy, filled with danger and adventure.

Perhaps the most remarkable of the Greeks' inventions was the drama. The Athenians wrote and performed the world's first plays, in open-air theatres set on a hillside.

The greatest Greek dramatists were Athenians such as Aeschylus and Sophocles, but theatres spread all over the Greek world. The finest surviving theatre is at Epidaurus, where the ancient plays are still regularly performed.

Two Greeks, Herodotus and Thucydides, were the first true historians. They did not just record past events, but tried to check their information and explain why things had turned out as they did.

The Greeks were also the first philosophers — men who tried to understand the world without relying on accepted myths and traditions. One outstanding philosopher, Socrates, asked questions such as: 'What is the best kind of life?' and 'Why should we obey the government?' Many Athenians were so upset by Socrates' questionings that he was eventually condemned to death for supposedly insulting the gods. Socrates had a famous pupil, Plato — and Plato's pupil was Aristotle, the philosopher who became Alexander the Great's tutor.

Below *A group of great philosophers and poets, (from left to right), Sophocles, Herodotus, Homer, Socrates, Plato, Aeschylus and Aristotle.*

The Olympic Games

Olympia in the Peloponnese (southern Greece) was a great religious centre, sacred to Zeus, king of the gods. The temple at Olympia housed a huge ivory and gold statue of the god, the master-work of the sculptor Phidias. It was thought to be one of the Seven Wonders of the Ancient World.

Every four years a festival was held at Olympia; it was so important in Greek life that warring states would declare a truce while it lasted. The high point of the festival was the five-day Olympic Games, to which competitors flocked from the Greek city-states — even those in far-away southern Italy and Sicily. Chariot and horse racing, running, jumping, throwing the discus and javelin, wrestling and boxing were contested by athletes who had trained for at least ten months beforehand.

Victory in the Games was rewarded with a simple olive crown. The glory an athlete might win for himself and his city was immense — even greater than a modern gold

Above *An athlete with the ribbon of victory around his head.* **Below** *The Olympic games were held in honour of Zeus, every four years, when athletes competed in all kinds of sport.*

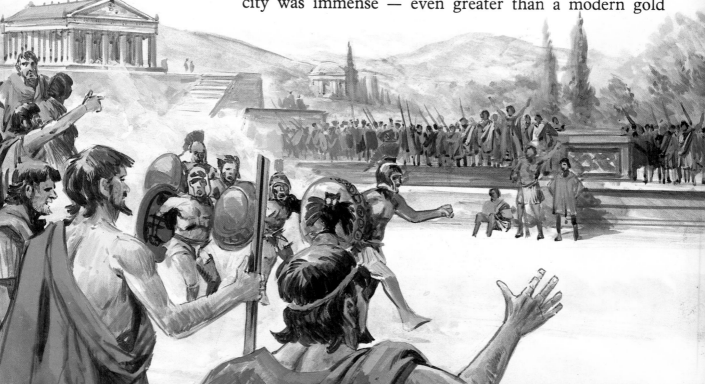

medallist enjoys, since the Greek 'medallist' shone with something of the splendour of Zeus himself, and would be celebrated in the verses of great poets.

The original Olympic Games are said to have begun in 776 BC. If so, they lasted for over a thousand years, until they were abolished in AD 339 by a Christian emperor determined to end the worship of Zeus. The modern Games were started by a French sportsman, Baron de Coubertin, in 1896.

Above *The seated figure of a boxer. On his left hand you can see the leather thongs and strap which protect his hands and wrists.* **Left** *A discus thrower.*

5 THE GREEK WAY OF LIFE

Ideals of excellence

The Greeks loved excellence, but they insisted that the complete man must combine several important qualities of mind and body. The ideal was not the specialist — not even the great philosopher or athlete — but the 'all-round man' who was capable of being good company at a banquet, taking part intelligently in public affairs, or fighting effectively in the ranks.

Greek education was designed to produce such a man,

Below *Greek children learned to read from writing on waxed blocks. The wax was marked using a sharp wooden instrument called a stylus.*

but not such a woman. Women were treated quite differently. Poor children probably began helping their fathers and mothers on the farm or in the workshop from an early age. But the children of wealthier parents were taught at home by a household slave, the pedagogus, and then the boys went to school — or rather, to three schools!

At the grammar school they learned to write, practising with a stylus (a pointed stick) on a wax block that could be wiped clean and re-used; then they went on to study the Greek literary classics. At a separate music school they learned to play the lyre or the flute. And at a physical training school they were kept fit and taught dancing.

A Greek boy might learn other skills from a private tutor, if his family could afford one. From the fourth century BC he might also get a 'higher education' in Athens at the Academy founded by the philosopher Plato.

Below *A pair of bronze compasses.*

Below *Music was an important part of a Greek boy's education. They learned to play the lyre and pipes.*

Above *Slaves working in the silver mines.* **Opposite** *A slave fastens her mistress's sandal. This piece of sculpture is from a tomb of the fourth century* BC.

Citizens and slaves

The Greek city-states varied greatly in size, customs and organization. Sparta, for example, was unique in having a well-trained full-time army and a large and mutinous helot population.

Oligarchies generally limited political rights (for example, the right to vote) to wealthy people. In a democracy such as Athens, all citizens had equal rights. All important decisions were made by the Assembly, which consisted of all citizens who cared to turn up. It met in the agora (market place) of the city about every ten days.

Good speakers inevitably wielded exceptional influence in the Assembly, and the rich still tended to play an important part, since they had the time and money to give to politics. Rich and poor also made different contributions to the state. In Athens, the wealthier citizens became soldiers in time of war, while the poorest rowed the galleys in the fleet.

In any city-state, only about one person in six was a citizen. Women, children and foreign residents had no political rights; and slaves had few rights of any kind. It is hard for us to understand how Athenian democrats could tolerate slavery, but in fact all Greeks accepted it. People fell into slavery for a lot of different reasons. Children who were abandoned by their parents became the slaves of the people who brought them up. In war the soldiers who were captured were often sold into slavery.

However, the number of slaves was relatively small, and the Athenians seem never to have feared them as the Spartans feared their helots. Given the very simple Greek way of life, most slaves were probably little different from farm workers or servants — except those unfortunate enough to be sent to dig in the silver mines. These slaves were often branded and chained together, and worked long shifts in the small dark tunnels. They had little hope of freedom.

House and home

The Greeks put a great amount of energy into public life and believed it to be very important. One sign of this was the way in which they made their temples and public buildings of marble, yet used only humble clay bricks for their own homes. However, the Greek house was a very private place. It was plain and uninviting at the front, with very small windows. The centre of household activity was further back, in rooms arranged round an inner courtyard. Even today, many Mediterranean houses follow the same plan.

Greek men spent a lot of their time away from home, either at work or at leisure. The house was the woman's

The Greek home was a hive of industry. The women of the household provided for all the family needs.

realm — and also something that could almost be called her prison. Apart from shopping at the market in the city, a wife was expected to spend most of her time out of sight, in the home. When guests arrived for a meal, the men ate together, while the women stayed apart in their own quarters. The Greeks' attitude towards women was an arrogant one: the ideal woman, according to Pericles, was the one who attracted the least attention.

A woman could not inherit or hold property, or become involved in any business deal worth more than a bushel of grain. But within the house, a wife had authority over her children and the slaves, if she had any. She was responsible for cooking, housework, and spinning and weaving the cloth for the family's clothing. If her husband was a farmer — and most Greeks were — the sheep would provide wool and the crops would provide food. The average Greek household thus produced for itself most of what it needed to survive.

Above *Two potters work on a huge storage jar. The fine Greek pottery was produced for wealthy people to use, while the ordinary people used pottery of a much rougher kind.*

Farmers and craftsmen

Most Greeks were farmers. Greece was not a very fertile country, since it was criss-crossed by mountain ranges, with only small areas of valley and plain suitable for cultivation. Poor pasture meant that goats rather than cows were raised in most places. But oxen were needed for ploughing. Large numbers of sheep were also kept, first for wool and secondly for meat. The staple crops were cereals, and most ordinary people's meals consisted of porridge, with olives, goat's milk, cheese and figs.

Some areas — notably Attica, the territory around Athens — went over to vine and olive growing on a large scale. Wine and oil became Athenian exports which helped to make the city rich — and also made it necessary to produce thousands of storage jars. The Greeks' achievements as potters and vase painters would hardly have been so great if it had not been for the trade in oil and wine.

Most farms were family holdings, supporting a household which perhaps included two or three slaves. Greek states were so small that such farms were only a few miles from the city, enabling the farmer to walk in and play his part in public affairs.

Apart from the great buildings on the acropolis, everything in the city was also on a small scale. The houses were cramped together in crooked little streets where craftsmen and shopkeepers ran individual businesses. Even the Parthenon was built by many independent craftsmen. Athens had only one 'factory', where over a thousand slaves made shields, and one great 'industry' — a silver mine that largely financed the war against Persia.

Below *Greek farmers' families could survive entirely on their own produce from the land and river — cheese, bread, vegetables, olives, fish and wine.*

Clothes, fashion and leisure

Greek dress was very simple, and varied little over centuries. The main garment was a tunic, the chiton, consisting of a rectangle of material wrapped round the body or fastened with a pin. Men's tunics were short, while women wore them ankle-length. On occasion a cloak, the himation, was worn over the chiton. The clothes were often dyed very bright colours.

However, the Greeks were certainly interested in their appearance, and by the Classical period there were all sorts of beauty aids. Fashions came and went in the way hair and beards were styled, and Athenian men seem to have gone to the hairdresser's often, using the shop as a

Below *There were always great entertainments at banquets including acrobats and dancers.*

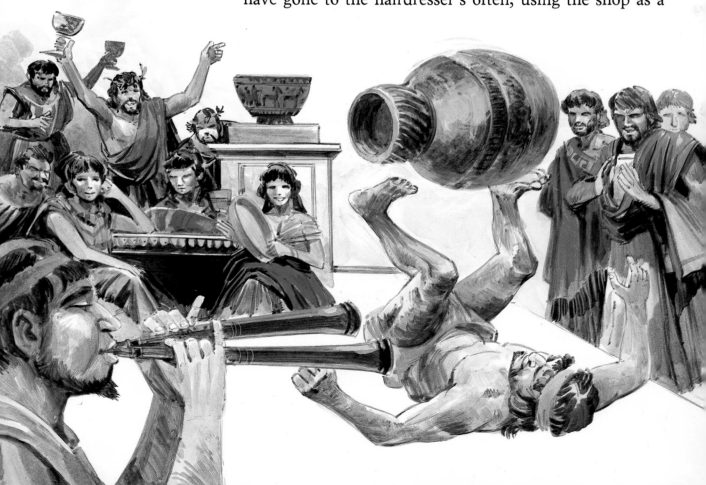

sort of club. For women, cosmetics, perfumes, jewellery and wigs were on sale in the agora at Athens. Just as they do today, comic writers made rude jokes about the silliness of fashions without managing to put anyone off them!

Greek men visited the gymnasium regularly, working out on a sanded training ground before retiring to the baths, which resembled the modern sauna. Another favourite leisure activity was dining with friends. The dinner — or, for the wealthy, the banquet — could be quite elaborate, with libations to the gods, recitations and songs. There would also be performances by professional acrobats and dancers. Unfortunately almost nothing is known about the music that was played.

The Greeks played ball games, dice, and even a game that has survived right down to the present which is called 'fives' (five-stones).

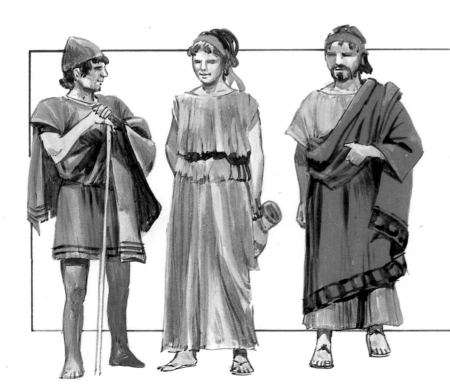

Above *Ancient Greek mirrors were nearly always discs of polished bronze on top of small bronze statues.*

Left *Both Greek men and women wore simple clothes consisting of a tunic, called a chiton. The man on the right is wearing a cloak, called an himation.*

Above *A phalanx of Greek infantrymen. A phalanx was a formation of soldiers in battle, in which the soldiers created a wall of overlapping shields.*

Below *A vase design showing Achilles and Memnon, the king of Ethiopia, fighting.*

Waging war

There were frequent wars between the Greek city-states, but only the Spartans could be called full-time soldiers. In most other states, all young citizens did some military training and were liable to be called up if war broke out. At Athens, citizens who could afford the equipment (helmet, shield, breastplate, shinguard, spear) joined the army as hoplites, heavy-armed spearmen. Poorer citizens, thetes, served as oarsmen in the fleet.

The Greeks were excellent soldiers. They observed discipline so well that their infantry formation, the phalanx, was highly manoeuvrable in attack and rock-steady in defence. Having defeated the Persians, Greek soldiers were in great demand as mercenaries who fought for pay. The Persian king hired many of them, and in several battles they provided the toughest opposition to Alexander the Great. On these occasions, as so often, Greek fought Greek.

During the classical age the infantry dominated Greek military strategy. Cavalry units were quite small, since horses were expensive to maintain and therefore few in number. This was not the case in Macedon, and Philip and Alexander developed a formidable Macedonian cavalry which changed the nature of warfare. The phalanx played its part in Alexander's victories, but cavalry made them far more complete than the military successes of Athens or Sparta: cavalry could turn an enemy's flank, cut off his retreat, or pursue and destroy him when he broke and ran.

Below *A fully armed hoplite (infantryman). Under his tunic he wears a bronze breast plate and on his legs he wears greaves to protect his shins. a) a hoplite's bronze helmet. The plumes on hoplites' helmets were made of dyed horsehair; b) a cavalryman's helmet; c) a double-edged, and a single-edged sword.*

Ships and sailors

The Greeks had a long tradition of seamanship. They fished, traded and fought on the water with vigour, despite the fact that ancient navigation and equipment were too primitive for long voyages on the open sea to be safe. Much of Homer's great poem the *Odyssey* describes the adventures of the Greek hero Odysseus and his men, who are blown off course and wander from one strange place to another at the mercy of wind and waves. Understandably, the Greeks — like their other great

rivals, the Phoenicians — sailed as close as they could to the coast even while trading and colonizing all round the Mediterranean.

Merchant ships were mainly driven by sail, but warships had both sails and banks (rows) of oars, for it was the strenuous rowing of oarsmen that gave the ship the speed it needed in battle. A ram on the front of the ship was the main offensive weapon, designed to sink or cripple the enemy's ships.

The classic Athenian warship was the trireme — that is, a vessel with three banks of oars and oarsmen, arranged one above the other. This meant that about 170 oarsmen could operate on a ship that was not much more than 100 feet (30 metres) long. So Athenian warships were compact, fast and effective fighting machines, manned by citizen oarsmen (thetes) and capable of defeating the combined Persian and Phoenician fleets.

Above *In Homer's* Odyssey *Odysseus and his crew were lured into a whirlpool on their dangerous return journey to Ithaca.*

6 THE HELLENISTIC AGE

The end of an era

Below *Demosthenes, an Athenian orator.*

During the fourth century BC the Greek city-states remained as quarrelsome and disunited as ever. At the same time, they showed a slackening of spirit. Ordinary Greeks began to lose their taste for soldiering, and the city-states relied increasingly for protection on the dubious loyalty of mercenary troops.

This made it easier for Philip of Macedon to take control of Greece. By a mixture of diplomacy and force, Philip isolated his enemies and removed them one after another. A famous Athenian orator, Demosthenes,

repeatedly warned the Greeks of Philip's ambitions. But when the Thebans and Athenians finally acted together, it was too late. Philip defeated them decisively at the battle of Chaeronaea in 338 BC.

After this, the city-states became unwilling, barely independent allies of Philip, and later of his son Alexander. They played a supporting role in Alexander's wars, but he never trusted them and they detested him as a tyrant. They reluctantly recognized him as a god — and rejoiced when he died.

However, the city-states never regained their lost greatness. The classical age is generally thought to have ended with the death of Alexander in 323 BC. The new age — the Hellenistic age — was quite different in atmosphere.

Above *The battle of Chaeronaea*

Above *A coin showing the head of Philip of Macedon.*

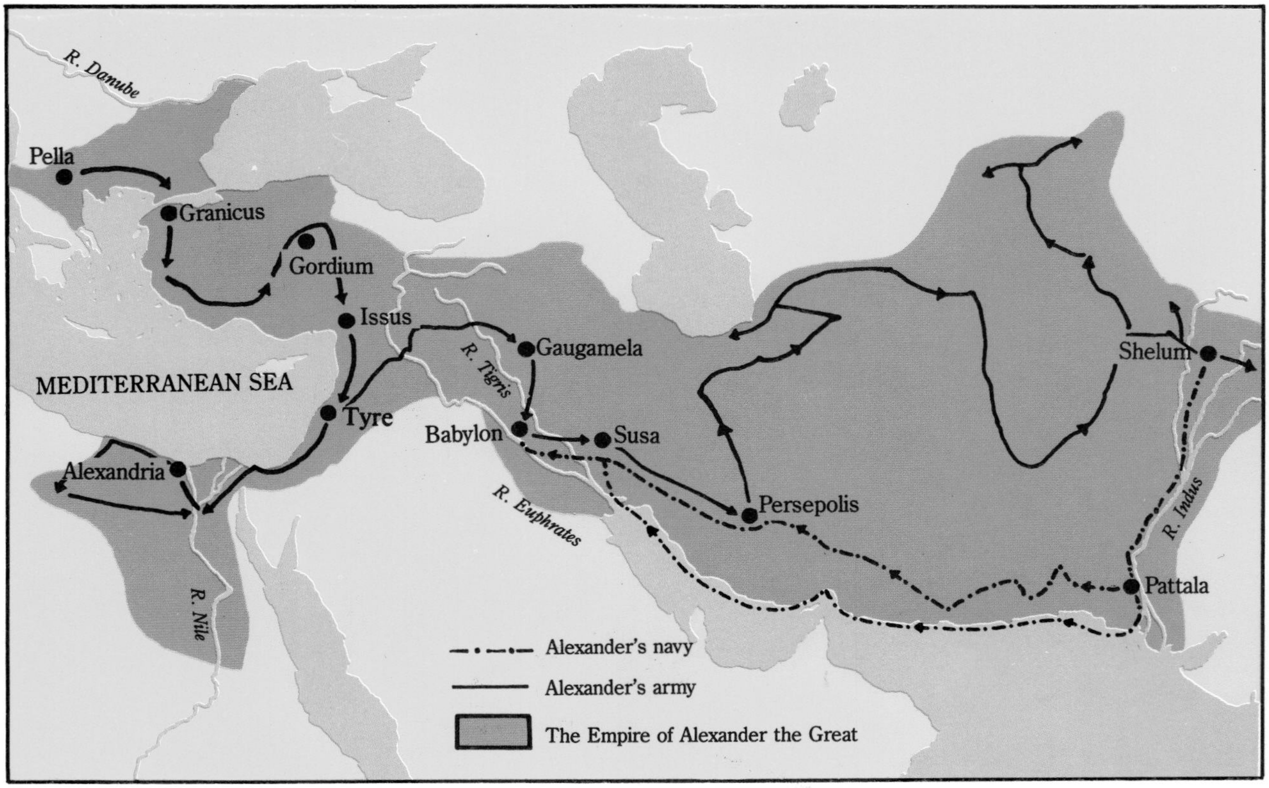
R. Danube
Pella
Granicus
Gordium
Issus
Gaugamela
MEDITERRANEAN SEA
R. Tigris
Tyre
Babylon
Susa
Alexandria
R. Euphrates
Persepolis
R. Nile
Shelum
R. Indus
Pattala
Alexander's navy
Alexander's army
The Empire of Alexander the Great

Above *The map shows the limits of Alexander's empire and the movements of his army and navy.*

The Greek East

When Alexander died, he left behind him no son old enough to rule. His vast empire was quickly divided between his best generals, who became the kings of Macedon, western Asia and Egypt. However, this meant that control remained with Greek rulers, and the Greek language and outlook spread all round the eastern Mediterranean. So the result of Alexander's conquests was a great enlargement of the Greek world.

Macedon, the Seleucid Empire of western Asia, and

Egypt were the great powers of the Hellenistic world. Athens and the city-states lived on, and even remained theoretically independent, but they were no longer politically or economically important. In fact Athens became a sort of museum-city, visited by tourists who admired her great past. The living centres of Greek literature, science and art were outside mainland Greece, in places such as Alexandria in Egypt.

By the second century BC a new power was making itself felt in the Mediterranean — Rome. Macedon and the rest of Greece had come under Roman rule by 146 BC, and eventually Rome absorbed the entire Greek East. But it remained Greek-speaking, and the Romans themselves were 'conquered' by Greek culture, which became the mark of an educated man everywhere in the Roman world. Through the Romans, the best achievements of the Greeks were passed on to our own civilization.

Below *During the second century BC the power of Rome became stronger and stronger. Gradually parts of the Greek empire were taken over by the Romans.*

7 OUR DEBT TO THE GREEKS

Our western civilization developed after the collapse of the Roman Empire, but its main inspiration was the achievement of the Greeks and Romans. Even until quite recent times, Greek and Latin were considered the most important subjects in many schools! And at every stage of western history, when people have felt at a loss for new ideas, they have looked back for them in the history of these brilliant civilizations.

Politically, we owe our most vital ideas to the Greeks: the actual words 'politics' and 'democracy' are taken from Greek. In a world where authority was based on tradition or brute force, Greek thinkers dared to ask why governments should be obeyed and what purpose they should serve. Some of these thinkers concluded that the state should exist for the benefit of its citizens, and therefore they should take part in running it.

The pioneering efforts of the Greeks in philosophy, drama, science, history and art have already been outlined. They were all part of a Greek view of life which emphasized the nobility and excellence that human beings might achieve. We are still struggling to achieve them.

This illustration shows the many different aspects of ancient Greek society — statesmanship, architecture, warfare, trade, drama (tragedy and comedy), medicine, art and craftsmanship.

Table of dates

BC

c **1900** First Greek-speaking peoples arrive in mainland Greece.

c **1450-1250** Mycenaean power at its height.

c **800** Homeric poems composed.

c **800-600** Greek colonies established in many parts of Mediterranean.

776 Olympic Games founded at Elis in southern Greece.

c **650-500** Age of tyrants.

546 Persians conquer Ionia.

508 Athens becomes a democracy.

499-494 Unsuccessful revolt of Ionian cities against Persians.

490 Invading Persians defeated by Athenians at Marathon.

480 Greek fleet defeats Persians at Salamis.

479 Greeks defeat Persian army at Plataea and navy at Mycale. End of Persian threat.

478 Formation of the Delian League.

449 End of war against Persia.

431-404 Peloponnesian War between Athens and Sparta.

415-413 Disastrous Athenian expedition to Syracuse.

405 Athenian fleet destroyed at Aegospotomi.

404 Surrender of Athens to Spartans.

371 Spartans defeated at Leuctra by Thebans under Epaminondas.

362 Battle of Mantinea: Epaminondas killed, Theban supremacy ended.

356 Philip II becomes king of Macedon. Alexander the Great born.

338 Philip defeats Athens and Thebes at Chaeronaea. Alexander in exile.

337 Alexander reconciled with Philip.

336 Macedonian advance force lands in Asia Minor. Philip murdered. Alexander becomes king of Macedon.

335 Thebes revolts and is destroyed by Alexander.

334 Alexander invades Asia Minor, wins battle of the Granicus.

333 Alexander defeats Darius at battle of Issus.

332 Alexander besieges and captures Tyre; crowned pharaoh at Memphis in Egypt.

331 Alexander defeats Darius at Gaugamela.

330 Darius murdered.

330-327 Alexander's conquest of eastern Persia.

327-325 Alexander's campaigns in India.

323 Alexander dies at Babylon, aged 32.

146 Greece becomes a Roman province.

Glossary

Acropolis The citadel or fortified hilltop of a city. The inhabitants could take refuge in the acropolis when the city was attacked.

Agora Open area in a city, used as a market-place and for public assemblies.

Chiton Tunic worn by Greek men and women.

Classical Term used to describe the great age of the Greek city-states, *c* 500-323 BC, and the art produced by them.

Exile An enforced absence from one's home country.

Galley Ship propelled by large numbers of oarsmen.

Hellenistic This describes the period of Greek history from the death of Alexander to the Roman conquest of Greece. It also describes the art of the period.

Helots Serfs or slaves, the great majority of the population in the Spartan state. Their labour supported the Spartans, who did no work but formed a warrior caste holding down the helots.

Himation Cloak worn by Greeks.

Hoplite Heavy-armed spearman. In Athens the better-off or 'middle' class served as hoplites.

Libation An offering to the gods in the form of wine or some other liquid.

Lyre Musical instrument with strings, played by plucking similar to a small harp.

Migration The movement of people from one place to settle in another.

Mycenaean This describes the Greeks of the period down to about 1200 BC. It is the adjective of Mycenae, the chief fortress-city at that time.

Myth Popular story or legend about gods and similar supernatural subjects.

Oracle Place where a god or goddess was said to speak prophetically, usually through the mouth of a priest or priestess. The word 'oracle' can also be used to describe the priest, or the 'message'.

Phalanx Greek infantry formation. The arrangement of the phalanx changed over time.

Polis The Greeks' own name for the city-state. From it we get the word 'politics', and 'metropolis'.

Regent A person put in charge of ruling a country if the real leader is too young, ill, or far away to govern properly.

Satrap Governor of a Persian province.

Seleucid dynasty A line of kings who reigned over a large empire in western Asia from 312 to 64 BC.

Thetes The poorest class of citizens at Athens, which provided the oarsmen for the fleet. Because the Athenian fleet was so important, the thetes were able to gain political rights, making Athens a democracy.

Trireme Ancient type of ship, rowed by three banks of oarsmen.

Further information

Places to visit

Libraries Ask at your local library for further information about the Greeks. The librarians may be able to provide some of the books listed below, which are well worth reading.

Famous sites The remains of Greek civilization have been found in many parts of the Mediterranean. Among the most interesting are the temples at Paestum and Agrigento in Sicily, and the theatres at Ephesus and Pergamum in Turkey.

Entire books have been written about the sites in Greece itself! The most famous is of course the Acropolis at Athens, where the Parthenon and other wonderful temples still stand in ruined splendour. The theatre at Epidaurus and the ruins of Delphi, Olympia and other mainland sites are well worth visiting, as are Rhodes and other islands.

The earlier civilization of Crete can be studied on the island, notably at Knossos. In southern Greece, the massive walls and Lion Gate of Mycenae are an awe-inspiring sight.

Museums Many countries have museums containing at least some Greek objects — sculptures, metalwork, coins or pottery, for example. Some of the finest works of art are in museums such as the British Museum in London, the Louvre in Paris, and the Vatican Museums and Museo Diocleziano in Rome. In Athens, the National Archaeological Museum and Acropolis Museum contain many treasures, and each of the other important sites has its own museum.

Books

Brochard, Philippe, *Alexander the Great* (Granada, 1983)

Connolly, Peter, *The Greek Armies* (Macdonald Educational, 1977)

Cottrell, Leonard, *The Bull of Minos* (Evans, revised edition, 1962)

Cottrell, Leonard, *The Lion Gate* (Evans, 1966)

Crosher, Judith, *The Greeks* (Macdonald Educational, 1974)

Dover, Kenneth, *The Greeks* (BBC, 1980)

Fagg, Christopher, *Ancient Greece* (Longman, 1978)

Green, Peter, *Alexander the Great* (Weidenfeld, 1970)

Harris, Nathaniel, *The Greeks and Romans* (W.H. Smith, 1980)

Jones, John Ellis, *Ancient Greece* (Kingfisher Books, 1983)

Millard, Anne, *Ancient Greece* (Usborne, 1981) and *Ancient Greece* (Granada, 1982)

Purves, Amanda, *Growing up in Ancient Greece* (Wayland, 1978)

Stewart, Philippa, *Growing up in Ancient Greece* (Batsford)

Warner, Rex, *Men of Athens* (Bodley Head, 1972)

Index

Picture acknowledgements

The illustrations in this book were supplied by: The Mansell Collection 5, 11, 17, 35, 37, 39, 50, 51; The British Museum 29, 41, 46.